Dear Parent:
Your child's love of reading starts here!

Every child learns to read in a different way and at his or her own speed. You can help your young reader improve and become more confident by encouraging his or her own interests and abilities. You can also guide your child's spiritual development by reading stories with biblical values and Bible stories, like I Can Read! books published by Zonderkidz. From books your child reads with you to the first books he or she reads alone, there are I Can Read! books for every stage of reading:

SHARED READING
Basic language, word repetition, and whimsical illustrations, ideal for sharing with your emergent reader.

BEGINNING READING
Short sentences, familiar words, and simple concepts for children eager to read on their own.

READING WITH HELP
Engaging stories, longer sentences, and language play for developing readers.

READING ALONE
Complex plots, challenging vocabulary, and high-interest topics for the independent reader.

ADVANCED READING
Short paragraphs, chapters, and exciting themes for the perfect bridge to chapter books.

I Can Read! books have introduced children to the joy of reading since 1957. Featuring award-winning authors and illustrators and a fabulous cast of beloved characters, I Can Read! books set the standard for beginning readers.

A lifetime of discovery begins with the magical words **"I Can Read!"**

Visit www.icanread.com for information on enriching your child's reading experience.
Visit www.zonderkidz.com for more Zonderkidz I Can Read! titles.

A message came to Jonah from the Lord ...
He said, "Go to the great city of Nineveh.
Announce to its people the message I give you."
—*Jonah 3:1–2*

ZONDERKIDZ

Jonah, God's Messenger
Copyright © 2011 by Zondervan
Illustrations © 2011 by Dennis G. Jones

Requests for information should be addressed to:
Zondervan, *Grand Rapids, Michigan 49530*

Library of Congress Cataloging-in-Publication Data

Jonah, God's messenger.
   p. cm. — (I can read!)
  ISBN 978-0-310-71835-2 (softcover)
  1. Jonah (Biblical prophet)—Juvenile literature.
  BS580.J55J62 2011
  224'.9209505—dc22
                                              2010053408

Published in association with the literary agency of Alive Communications, Inc., 7680 Goddard Street #200, Colorado Springs, CO 80920. www.alivecommunications.com

Zonderkidz is a trademark of Zondervan.

Editor: Mary Hassinger

Printed in China

11 12 13 14 15 16 17 /SCC/ 7 6 5 4 3 2

JONAH
God's Messenger

pictures by Dennis G. Jones

Jonah was a prophet.

He loved God.

He told many people about God.

One day, God said to Jonah,

"Go to Nineveh.

It is a big city.

Tell the people to stop being bad."

But Jonah was not happy

about this job.

Jonah did not want to
help those people.
He ran away.
He made a plan to go
to Tarshish.

Tarshish was far away.

Jonah could not walk that far!

He bought a ticket

to go away on a boat.

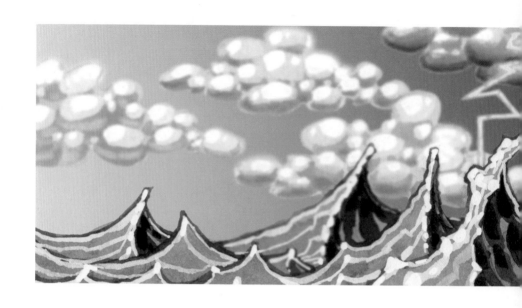

God did not want Jonah

to go to Tarshish.

He wanted Jonah to go

to Nineveh.

He knew how to stop Jonah.

God sent a BIG storm!

The storm and wind were strong!

All the men on the boat were scared.

But not Jonah!

He was asleep in the boat.

The men went to see Jonah.

"Wake up!" they all shouted.

Jonah woke up.

"Help us, Jonah!

Talk to your God.

Ask him what we should do.

We are scared," they all said.

Jonah knew what to do.

He thought, *I cannot run from God.*

Jonah told the men,

"Throw me into the water.

Then the storm and the wind

will be quiet."

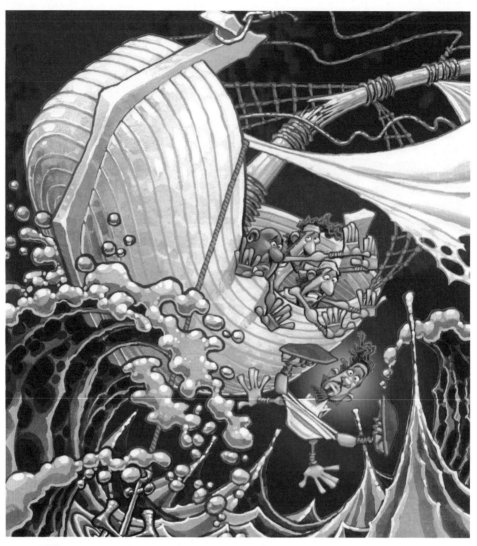

The men were scared.

But they did what Jonah said.

Jonah fell into the water

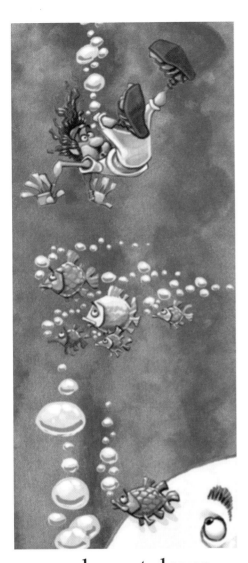
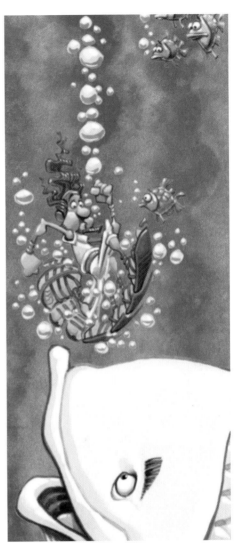

and went down,

down,

down ...

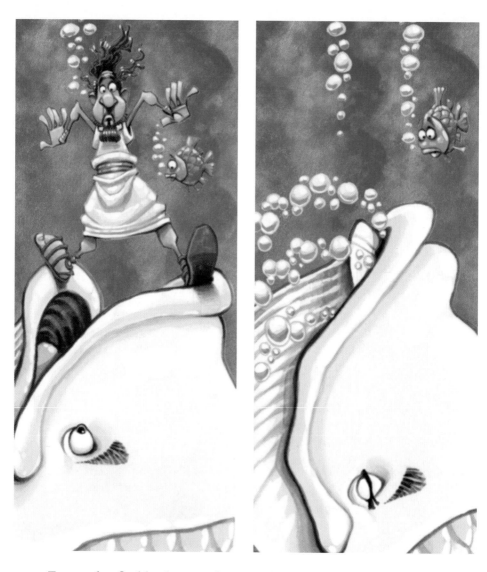

Jonah fell deep into the sea.

God sent a huge fish

to catch Jonah when he fell!

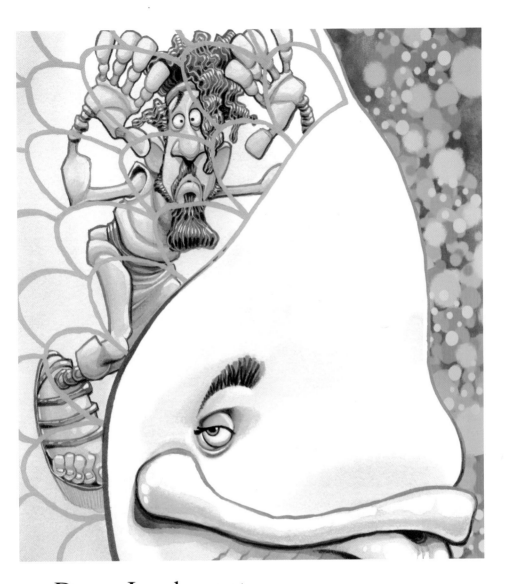

Down Jonah went …

right into the mouth of the huge fish.

GULP!

Jonah was in the big fish for

three days and three nights.

Jonah prayed and prayed,

"I am sorry, God.

I am ready to do my job."

So God told the big fish to
spit Jonah out!

Jonah landed on the shore.

He landed on dry land,

right where he needed to be.

29

Then God said to Jonah again,

"Go to Nineveh.

Tell the people about me.

Tell the people to be good!"

Jonah said, "OK, God. I will go."

Jonah told the people
in Nineveh about God.
The people believed Jonah.
They wanted to know more
about God.
God was happy with Nineveh,
and God was happy with Jonah!